# IT'S MY STATE! ★

# ALASKA

Ruth Bjorklund

William McGeveran

**Marshall Cavendish**
Benchmark
New York

Published by Marshall Cavendish Benchmark
An imprint of Marshall Cavendish Corporation

Website: www.marshallcavendish.us

This publication represents the opinions and views of the authors based on their personal experience, knowledge, and research. The information in this book serves as a general guide only. The authors and publisher have used their best efforts in preparing this book and disclaim liability rising directly and indirectly from the use and application of this book.

Other Marshall Cavendish Offices:
Marshall Cavendish International (Asia) Private Limited, 1 New Industrial Road, Singapore 536196 •
Marshall Cavendish International (Thailand) Co Ltd. 253 Asoke, 12th Flr, Sukhumvit 21 Road, Klongtoey Nua,
Wattana, Bangkok 10110, Thailand • Marshall Cavendish (Malaysia) Sdn Bhd, Times Subang, Lot 46, Subang
Hi-Tech Industrial Park, Batu Tiga, 40000 Shah Alam, Selangor Darul Ehsan, Malaysia

Marshall Cavendish is a trademark of Times Publishing Limited

All websites were available and accurate when this book was sent to press.

Library of Congress Cataloging-in-Publication Data
Bjorklund, Ruth.
   Alaska / Ruth Bjorklund, William McGeveran. — 2nd ed.
     p. cm. — (It's my state!)
   Includes bibliographical references and index.
   Summary: "Surveys the history, geography, government, economy, and people of Alaska"—Provided by publisher.
   ISBN 978-1-60870-655-6 (print) — ISBN 978-1-60870-810-9 (ebook)
   1. Alaska—Juvenile literature. I. McGeveran, William. II. Title.
 F904.3.B56 2013
 979.8—dc23            2011020744

Second Edition developed for Marshall Cavendish Benchmark by RJF Publishing LLC (www.RJFpublishing.com)
Series Designer, Second Edition: Tammy West/Westgraphix LLC
Editor, Second Edition: Emily Dolbear

All maps, illustrations, and graphics © Marshall Cavendish Corporation. Maps and artwork on pages 6, 30, 31, 75, 76, and back cover by Christopher Santoro. Map and graphics on pages 10 and 42 by Westgraphix LLC.

The photographs in this book are used by permission and through the courtesy of:
**Front cover:** Nomad/Superstock and Alaska Stock/Alamy (inset).
**Alamy:** Visual&WrittenSL, 5 (left); Alaska Stock, 12, 19, 25, 40, 54, 58, 71 (right); tbkmedia.de, 13; Blaine Harrington III, 15; Douglas Peebles Photography, 17; Picture Press, 18; Craig Lovell/Eagle Visions Photography, 22; John Elk III, 24; Everett Collection Inc., 29; Ellen McKnight, 34; Peter Arnold Inc., 43; Lawrence Migdale/PIX, 44; david sanger photography, 45; Accent Alaska.com, 53, 60, 68. **Associated Press:** Associated Press, 36, 49, 50, 61, 67, 70, 71 (left). **Corbis:** The Gallery Collection, 27; Vince Streano, 48; Alaska Stock, 56. **Getty Images:** Time & Life Pictures, 46; WireImage, 47 (left); Getty Images Entertainment, 47 (right). **Superstock:** IndexStock, 4 (left), 21 (left); Minden Pictures, 4 (right), 8, 16, 51; NaturePL, 5 (right); Richards Cummins, 9; age fotostock, 11, 62, 64, 65, 74; Robert Harding Picture Library, 20, 37; imagebroker.net, 21 (left), 52; Everett Collection, 33; Science Faction, 38.

Printed in Malaysia (T).
135642

# CONTENTS

## State Flower: Forget-Me-Not

A well-known native wildflower, the forget-me-not was the official flower of the "Golden Igloo," a group of early pioneers. Adopted by the Alaska Territory, it became the state flower when Alaska gained statehood. Forget-me-nots bloom on the tundra and throughout Alaska in June and July. The flowers, which range in color from pink, light blue, and white, have five petals and a yellow center.

## State Bird: Willow Ptarmigan

The willow ptarmigan is a relative of the Arctic grouse and lives in Alaska's tundra and high alpine areas. These birds like to eat willow tree buds and twigs. In the winter, their feathers are white to help them hide from predators in the snow. In the summer and fall, their feathers are brown to help them blend in with the ground and plants.

## State Tree: Sitka Spruce

In the rain forests of southeastern Alaska, Sitka spruce can grow to heights of 200 feet (60 meters) or more. They may live for 800 years. American Indians have used the tree to make totems, masks, charms, and other carvings. Today the wood is also used for houses, ships, and musical instruments.

## State Land Mammal: Moose

The moose is the largest member of the deer family. It can stand 7.5 feet (2.3 m) tall. Its partly flat antlers can grow to be 6 feet (1.8 m) wide. One moose can eat more than 40 pounds (18 kilograms) of twigs, bark, needles, tree roots, water plants, and willow and birch leaves each day.

## State Marine Mammal: Bowhead Whale

Bowhead whales swim under the winter ice. They use their heads to smash through the ice to breathe. These whales can grow to be 60 feet (18 m) long and can weigh 120,000 pounds (54,500 kg). The U.S. government has listed them as endangered. That means they are in danger of becoming extinct, or completely dying out.

## State Dog: Alaskan Malamute

In 2010, after a campaign by students at the Polaris K–12 School in Anchorage, the Alaskan malamute was named the state dog. These animals, which Alaska's early peoples first used thousands of years ago for hunting and hauling loads, have played a big role in Alaska history. They often serve as family pets, but they require a great deal of daily exercise.

# The Last Frontier

The great naturalist John Muir first saw Alaska's Glacier Bay in 1879. He called it a "picture of icy wildness." The same words could be used today to describe Alaska itself, with its unspoiled natural wonders. The name *Alaska* comes from the Native Aleut people's word *Alyeshka*, meaning "the great land." Without a doubt, Alaska is great in its vast extent, rugged beauty, and energetic people.

## A Vast State

Alaska is the biggest of the fifty states. It covers a land area of more than 570,000 square miles (1.5 million square kilometers), with more than 33,000 miles (53,000 kilometers) of shoreline. It is more than twice as big as Texas, which ranks second in size.

Within its borders lie an amazing array of mountains, rivers, glaciers, volcanoes, islands, tundra, and rain forests. Alaska has more than 3 million lakes and several major rivers, including the Copper River and the Yukon. Huge coastal mountain ranges in the east and

*Quick Facts*

**ALASKA BORDERS**

| | |
|---|---|
| **North** | Arctic Ocean<br>Beaufort Sea |
| **South** | Gulf of Alaska<br>Pacific Ocean<br>Canada |
| **East** | Canada |
| **West** | Bering Sea<br>Chukchi Sea<br>Pacific Ocean |

The Inside Passage, along the coast of southeastern Alaska, is noted for its scenic beauty.

southeast rise up from sea level. To the north, the remote Brooks Range is the northernmost tip of the Rocky Mountains. Permanently frozen earth, ice floes and icebergs, eerie Northern Lights, days when the sun shines well past midnight, and more are all part of Alaska's fantastic glory.

Most of Alaska is a peninsula in the northwest corner of North America. Two oceans, the Arctic and the Pacific, and three seas, the Bering, Chukchi, and Beaufort, surround the state on three sides. From the southwest corner of the Alaska peninsula, a long chain of islands, the Aleutian Islands, extends to the southwest for 1,200 miles (1,900 km). From the southeast corner of the peninsula, a strip of land stretches south along the Pacific coast. This strip is called the Alaska Panhandle. The state is often divided into five regions. They range from southeastern Alaska (the Panhandle) to the Arctic North.

## Southeastern Alaska

Southeastern Alaska is a narrow, mountainous region along the coast of the Pacific Ocean. Thick rain forests of Sitka spruce, hemlock, ponderosa pine, and western cedar cover the mountains. A group of 1,100 offshore islands creates a system of canals, fjords, and channels called the Inside Passage. Cruise ships, ferries, tankers, tugs, barges, container ships, and pleasure boats travel through these scenic and protected waterways.

Southeastern Alaska is generally warmer and wetter than the rest of the state. Most years, around 150 to 200 inches (380 to 500 centimeters) of rain or snow fall in the area. On the upper slopes of the mountains, snow falls year round. Rivers freeze and form glaciers that flow to the sea.

Aboard one of the many cruise ships that sail the waters of the Inside Passage, these tourists enjoy a close-up view of the Hubbard Glacier.

Alaska probably has about 100,000 glaciers in all, many of them in the southeast. They vary greatly in size. Only about 600 have names. The largest glacier in the southeast, the Malaspina Glacier, covers about 1,500 square miles (3,900 sq km).

### Quick Facts

**A STATE WITH NO COUNTIES**

All U.S. states are divided into counties, except for Louisiana (which is made up of parishes) and Alaska. Alaska is divided into eighteen organized "boroughs." Each has its own local government. Although most of Alaska's people live in these boroughs, they take up less than half of the state's land area. The rest of Alaska is one big unorganized borough. This area is mostly wilderness and does not have its own local government.

# Alaska Boroughs

JUNEAU CITY AND BOROUGH

WRANGELL CITY AND BOROUGH

KETCHIKAN GATEWAY BOROUGH

HAINES BOROUGH

SKAGWAY MUNICIPALITY

SITKA CITY AND BOROUGH

YAKUTAT CITY AND BOROUGH

FAIRBANKS NORTH STAR BOROUGH

MATANUSKA-SUSITNA BOROUGH

DENALI BOROUGH

ANCHORAGE MUNICIPALITY

KENAI PENINSULA BOROUGH

NORTH SLOPE BOROUGH

NORTHWEST ARCTIC BOROUGH

KODIAK ISLAND BOROUGH

LAKE AND PENINSULA BOROUGH

BRISTOL BAY BOROUGH

ALEUTIANS EAST BOROUGH

**Alaska has 18 units of government called "boroughs" (including 2 municipalities). The rest of the state is 1 "unorganized borough."**

If you were to travel north through the Inside Passage, you would begin in the rain forests near the Misty Fjords National Monument. There, fog floats over narrow seas and steep cliffs. You would end your journey surrounded by icebergs and glaciers in Glacier Bay National Park. In geologic time, Glacier Bay is very new. Just over two hundred years ago, when British captain George Vancouver first sailed the area, he saw only "compact solid mountains of ice." Today, the glacier has melted to form a bay about 65 miles (105 km) long.

Most of the Panhandle, outside of Glacier Bay National Park, is taken up by the Tongass National Forest. Covering 16.8 million acres (6.8 million hectares), this temperate rain forest is bigger than the whole state of West Virginia. It is the country's largest national forest by far.

## South-Central Alaska

More than half of the state's people live in south-central Alaska, which includes much of the Alaska peninsula's southern coast and land north of the coast. There, you will find snow-covered mountain ranges, seas bursting with marine life, busy fishing communities, farmlands, national parks, and the municipality of Anchorage, the state's largest city in population. Huge amounts of precipitation fall, forming numerous glaciers. One glacier, the Bering, is bigger than the entire state of Rhode Island.

Two out of every five Alaskans live in the municipality of Anchorage.

Dall sheep have survived for thousands of years roaming Alaska's rugged mountain terrain.

Wrangell–St. Elias National Park, located in south-central Alaska, is the biggest of Alaska's eight national parks and the largest in the United States. Inside the park, the St. Elias Mountains link with the Wrangell, Alaska, and Chugach mountain ranges. Brown bears, mountain goats, Dall sheep, bison, and other wild creatures roam the parkland, which covers 13.2 million acres (5.3 million ha).

Kenai Fjords, on the Kenai Peninsula, is the smallest of Alaska's national parks. There, more than 400 inches (1,000 cm) of snow fall each year on mountains, glaciers, and a sheet of ice called the Harding Icefield. The Harding Icefield covers 300 square miles (775 sq km). The peninsula and the Gulf of Alaska are home to whales, seals, otters, and sea lions. Puffins, murres, and other seabirds also live there. Hardy mammals such as mountain goats, moose, bears, wolverines, and marmots live near the edges of the ice field.

## Western Alaska

Western Alaska includes the Aleutian Islands and Kodiak Island off Alaska's southwest coast, and the region extends northward along the west side of the Alaska peninsula. It is usually considered to stretch as far north as the Seward Peninsula on the west coast, just below the Arctic Circle.

Western Alaska is rich in wildlife. The wildlife refuge on Kodiak Island and nearby small islands is the only place in the world where you will find the Kodiak brown bear, the largest bear in the world. As many as 30 million seabirds migrate through this area. They include Emperor geese, murres, kittiwakes, cormorants, auklets, and puffins.

The Aleutians are a string of treeless, windswept islands. They stretch across the icy Bering Sea and North Pacific Ocean toward Russia. After leaving the busy Aleutian fishing port of Dutch Harbor, mariners sail over waters brimming with killer whales, gray whales, Steller sea lions, porpoises, and all five species of Pacific salmon. Many of the mountains are active volcanoes, such as those in the region called "Valley of Ten Thousand Smokes."

Brown bears are found throughout Alaska. Adults can weigh 900 pounds (400 kg) or more.

The 19-million-acre (8-million-ha) Yukon Delta National Wildlife Refuge, on Alaska's west coast, is the biggest wildlife refuge in the world. Across a broad plain in Western Alaska flow two of Alaska's greatest rivers, the Yukon—the state's longest river—and the Kuskokwim. As they spill into the sea, both rivers form enormous deltas, or networks of streams, inlets, and deposits of rock and sediment. The area around these two river deltas also has more than 40,000 lakes. It is a wonderland for waterfowl.

North of these deltas, the Seward Peninsula juts across the Bering Strait. It ends only 56 miles (90 km) from Siberia in eastern Russia. The historic village of Nome rests on the southern coast of the peninsula, overlooking Norton Sound. On the north side, soaring sea cliffs, lagoons, lava beds, and hot springs are home to waterfowl and birds of prey such as bald eagles, hawks, falcons, and owls.

## The Interior

The Interior of Alaska is immense. The region begins at the Canadian border in the east and sweeps west to the Yukon Delta. It is bordered to the south by the Alaska Range and to the north by the Brooks Range.

The central part of the Interior is mostly tundra. The land is flat, treeless, and cold. Great rivers flow through the Interior, among them the Yukon, Kuskokwim, Tanana, Porcupine, Koyukuk, and Innoko. The Tanana flows past Fairbanks, the region's major city. In the Interior wilderness, salmon swim up rivers to breed, and giant trumpeter swans and rare sandhill cranes spend summers raising their

*Quick Facts*

### ONE MOUNTAIN, TWO NAMES
Alaska's Native peoples called the region's tallest mountain *Denali*, meaning "the Great One" or "the High One." Later settlers named it Mount McKinley shortly before William McKinley was elected president in 1896. Alaska officially restored the original name in the 1970s, and the national park created in the area in 1980 was named Denali as well. The U.S. government still officially uses the name Mount McKinley, however.

Mount McKinley, or Mount Denali, is the highest mountain in all of North America. This aerial view shows its icy North Peak.

young. Caribou, moose, bears, lynx, and wolves make their homes on the tundra, on mountain slopes, or in forests of birch, spruce, and aspen.

Mount McKinley, also known as Mount Denali, in the Alaska Range is the tallest point in all of North America. At 20,320 feet (6,194 m), it towers over the other peaks in the range and can be seen 200 miles (320 km) away. Climbers first reached the summit in 1913. Nowadays, several hundred people make it to the top each year.

## The Arctic North

Northern Alaska looks cold and bleak, but it is full of life. Lying north of the Arctic Circle, the Brooks Range runs east to west across the southern border of Alaska's Arctic North region. The range is the northern tip of the continental divide and contains two national parks, Kobuk Valley and Gates of the Arctic. The peaks are jagged. "They go straight up and then straight down, like shark's teeth," says one truck driver, "and then it's flat all the way [north] to the sea." Rivers that flow from the Brooks Range are some of the wildest and most unspoiled in the world.

Spruce, fir, and pine trees grow on the south slope of the range. But because an average of no more than 10 inches (25 cm) of precipitation falls each year on the north side of the range, the region to the north known as the North Slope is

A barrier to winds from the Gulf of Alaska, the Alaska Range sometimes experiences cold weather.

nearly barren of trees. Scrubby shrubs, mosses, wildflowers, and lichens grow on the tundra. Underneath the surface soil of the tundra is a layer of permafrost, or permanently frozen earth. It cannot hold water, so plants with deep root systems cannot survive.

When the short Arctic spring comes, the snow and ice melt, and pools of water form above the permafrost layer. Wildflowers and grasses burst forth. Musk oxen, brown bears, foxes, wolves, and caribou, as well as birds from all over the world, move about the tundra. Along the coastline, rare marine mammals live among ice floes and along the coastal plain. They include Pacific walruses, polar bears, and bearded, ringed, and spotted seals, as well as beluga and gray whales, killer whales, and harbor porpoises.

## Climate and Seasons

The coldest temperature ever recorded in the United States—minus 80 degrees Fahrenheit (minus 62 degrees Celsius)—was measured at Prospect Creek Camp in Alaska's Brooks Range, on January 23, 1971. The average January temperature in Fairbanks is –10 °F (–23 °C). But the weather in Alaska is not as cold as many people think, at least in the southeast and south-central regions. There, the Pacific Ocean has a warming effect, and the Alaska Range blocks many cold, northerly winds. Temperatures range from around 20 °F (–7 °C) in winter to around 60 °F (16 °C) in summer.

Like the Aleutian Islands, the southern coastal areas are very wet. But the Aleutian Islands are colder, and the skies overhead are gray and cloudy on an average of 355 days a year.

Surrounded by mountain ranges, Alaska's Interior has the most dramatic weather contrasts. During the summer, long days and sunny skies can raise temperatures above 90 °F (32 °C). In the winter, when days average only four hours of light, the temperature can drop to around –60 °F (–50 °C). The weather is fairly dry. Only about 12 inches (30 cm) of precipitation falls each year.

The Arctic region is even drier. Scientists call the area a frozen desert. The Arctic Ocean ices over in winter, as do the rivers flowing across the tundra, and

The sun sets at the end of a warm summer day in Sitka, on the Alaskan Panhandle.

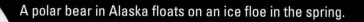

A polar bear in Alaska floats on an ice floe in the spring.

a massive sheet of ice blankets the region. Winter temperatures average around –20 °F (–30 °C). Added wind chills can make it feel like –60 °F (–50 °C) or lower. Even during the summer months, temperatures in the Arctic North rarely get above 50 °F (10 °C).

In Alaska, the summer solstice, or longest day of the year, and the winter solstice, or shortest day, are more than just dates on the calendar. At the Arctic Circle, the sun does not set during the summer solstice or rise during the winter solstice. Above the Arctic Circle this is true for a longer period of time.

In the northern Alaskan city of Barrow, for example, the summer sun stays in the sky, day and night, for eighty-four days. Even below the Arctic Circle, summer days are long. In Anchorage, the sun sets well after 10 P.M. on most summer nights. Alaskans love their long, light-filled summer days. But winter days are short, when there is any daylight at all. Barrow is without daylight for sixty-seven days each winter. People say that if you make it through an Alaskan winter, you deserve an Alaskan summer.

Spring in Alaska is big news. The season, like autumn, is very short, but it arrives with a bang. Along the Arctic coastline, the sea ice melts and splits into pieces called pack ice. These big ice floes provide the main hunting ground for polar bears. Elsewhere in Alaska, melting snow builds up huge amounts of slush and mud. Frozen rivers crack and thaw, sending water and chunks of ice downstream. Alaskans call the season "break up."

Spring and autumn are the best times of year to look for the Northern Lights, or aurora borealis. This amazing event happens when electrically charged particles from the Sun enter the atmosphere above the polar regions. The gases in the atmosphere react by flashing colored beams of light across the northern sky.

## KING OF THE SEA

The king, or chinook, salmon is Alaska's state fish. The biggest of all Pacific salmon, these fish generally weigh more than 30 pounds (14 kg). Like other salmon, they hatch in streams and travel to the ocean to live most of their life. Then, they return to their birthplace, where the females spawn, or lay thousands of eggs. After that, they die.

## In the Wild

Alaska has more wild caribou than people. The state is also home to wolves, musk oxen, Dall sheep, sea otters, river otters, loons, snowy owls, and trumpeter swans. Some animals that are endangered or threatened (at risk of becoming endangered) in the lower forty-eight states thrive in Alaska. They include the bald eagle, gray wolf, brown bear, and lynx. Migratory birds, such as the Arctic tern—which flies all the way from the South Pole each year—visit Alaska every summer to nest and feed. The waters of the state are rich habitats for polar bears, walruses, Pacific salmon, king crab, many types of seals, and beluga, humpback, and gray whales.

Yet even with Alaska's small population and vast areas of untouched wilderness, there are still threatened or endangered species in the state. Birds such as the short-tailed albatross and the Eskimo curlew are in danger of being lost forever. As a result of hunting, fishing, and pollution, marine mammals such as the Steller sea lion and five species of whales are also endangered.

The endangered short-tailed albatross makes its home in Japan but flies as far as Alaska to feed in the rich Arctic waters. A century ago, there were millions of these giant seabirds. Now just a few hundred remain. As commercial fishers toss their fishing lines overboard, the albatross dive for the bait and get tangled in the lines or snagged by the hooks. Fishers have started attaching noisy streamers to the gear to scare the birds away and help save their lives.

## Polar Bear

Polar bears live in the waters and pack ice of the Arctic region all around the world, including Alaska. (But there are no polar bears in Antarctica.) They have a keen sense of smell, sharp claws, strength, speed, and the camouflage of a white coat. These attributes help them hunt seals, walruses, whales, and birds. They are adapted to sea and can swim for hundreds of miles at a time. But a loss of sea ice as Earth's climate has gradually become warmer in recent years is shrinking their habitat. They are listed as a threatened species by the federal government.

## Walrus

Walruses live in shallow waters near land or on the ice along Alaska's coast. These huge marine mammals can weigh 2,000 pounds (900 kg) or more, and they have long canine teeth called tusks. They use them to crack breathing holes in the ice, attack polar bears and other predators, and pull their own huge bodies out of the water.

## Snowy Owl

Year round, snowy owls live on the open tundra. These large birds of prey nest on the ground. They hunt in the snow and over grassy meadows and marshlands. Snowy owls go after rodents, hares, songbirds, geese, and sometimes weasels and foxes.

## Caribou (Reindeer)

Caribou are well adapted to living on the tundra. Their hooves work like snowshoes and also help them swim and dig for food in the snow. When the snow melts, the hooves keep them from sinking into the mud. During spring and summer, caribou munch on the leaves of plants such as willows, sedges, and blueberries. In winter, they eat reindeer lichen.

## Reindeer Lichen

Reindeer lichen is a gray-green plant that grows across Alaska's tundra. Lichens are really two types of living things (fungi and algae) joined together. They do not have roots and need no soil to grow. To survive, the fungus part of the plant takes water out of the air, and the algae part makes energy from sunlight. Reindeer lichen is a favorite food for caribou, musk oxen, and moose.

## Fireweed

This wildflower is a common sight in Alaska, where it brightens up the short summer season. Each plant carries some 80,000 seeds. Fireweed grows and spreads in sunny areas opened up by construction or wildfires. When trees begin to take over, the seeds lie dormant in the ground, waiting for better growing conditions.

# From the Beginning

The history of Alaska is as colorful as the wildflowers that bloom on the tundra after the ground begins to thaw in the spring. Few states can match Alaska's long, amazing saga of ancient peoples and cultures, strong traditions, hardy explorers, and daring adventurers.

## Alaska's Early Peoples

When much of North America was covered by glaciers during the last Ice Age, the level of the sea was lower than today. About 11,000 to 30,000 years ago, scientists say, there was no Bering Strait (the body of water that now separates Siberia from Alaska where they are very near each other). Instead, there was a "land bridge," perhaps 1,000 miles (1,600 km) wide, between the continents of Asia and North America. This area is called Beringia. Prehistoric people from northern Asia settled there, following musk oxen, mammoths, mastodons, and other big game.

Most authorities think that, before the end of the last Ice Age, some of these hunters migrated by land into Alaska and beyond, perhaps traveling along the coast in an ice-free corridor. Among these hunters, it is believed, are the early ancestors of American Indians living in Alaska today.

When the Ice Age ended, the sea rose higher and flooded the land bridge. But most authorities believe that new waves of people arrived in the Alaska region

Some of Alaska's Native peoples are known for their skillfully carved totem poles.

## GIANTS OF ANCIENT ALASKA

The Alaska state fossil is the woolly mammoth, the largest member of the elephant family. Now extinct for 11,000 years, woolly mammoths once fed on tundra grasses. They stood 10 to 12 feet (3 to 3.7 m) tall at the shoulder and weighed as much as 16,000 pounds (7,500 kg).

over the next few thousand years. These people may have come across the Bering Sea by boat. Many believe that the Eskimos and Aleuts of today's Alaska are descended from these later arrivals. In any event, Eskimos and Aleuts are distinct ethnic groups, and they are not considered to be American Indians.

Among the American Indians in Alaska are three tribes that have lived along the coast of the Panhandle: the Haida, Tlingit, and Tsimshian. They belong to a group now called the Northwest Coast Indians. Many other Indians in this group live along the coasts of what is now western Canada and Washington State.

The early Indians along the Panhandle coast enjoyed mild weather year round. Lush rain forests supplied them with wood to make houses, carvings, tools, and boats. The men fished in rivers and seas filled with salmon. They often went to sea to raid rival villages. Their boats were dugout canoes, each one carved out of a single tree. The women gathered berries and roots. Ceremonies and feasts were colorful events. Craftsmen carved and painted masks. Women wove baskets and sewed fancy garments that included seeds, beads, shells, and feathers.

Other Indians lived inland on the Alaskan peninsula. These Indians, known as Athabascans, moved from place to place, usually following herds of caribou, moose, or other game. They made stone tools and weapons and, in the warmer months, lived in houses of bark that were easy to break up and transport. Besides hunting game, they caught salmon and freshwater fish and gathered berries. To prepare for the long, cold winters, they stored meat and moved into underground shelters.

Although Eskimos do not exchange greetings by rubbing noses, as some people think, they sometimes greet family and friends by placing the nose against the face.

Among other Native peoples were two Eskimo groups—the Inupiat and the Yup'ik. The Inupiat settled along the Arctic coastline. The men carved tools and hunting spears from ivory and bone. They fished, hunted waterfowl, and caught seals using narrow kayaks made from bone and hides. To capture whales and ivory-tusked walruses, they joined together in hunting parties. They used bigger, wider boats called umiaks. Women prepared food, made clothing, and tended their homes, made of whale bones and hides, driftwood, or snow. The Inupiat burned seal oil for fuel.

Living along Norton Sound, the Yup'ik Eskimos enjoyed a milder climate. They fished using hooks, spears, and nets, and they hunted ducks and birds.

The earliest Aleuts settled on the Aleutian Islands. They formed a society rich in art, religion, and community life. The climate was foggy, windy, and harsh, but the land did not freeze over, and food was plentiful. The men carved beautiful tools and weapons from bone and ivory. They fished with hooks and line and went to sea in kayaks made of bone and animal skin. Using harpoons, they hunted sea otters, hair seals, and sea lions. The women gathered berries and roots, and walked the beaches collecting mussels, clams, sea urchins, kelp, and seaweed. Big families of parents, children, and other relatives lived together in houses built underground. The women wove baskets and sewed sealskins into waterproof clothing.

## Quick Facts

### THEY LEFT THEIR NAMES

The Bering Strait and Bering Sea were named after Vitus Bering, who discovered that Siberia and North America were not connected by land. The Steller sea lion and Steller's jay, as well as the extinct Steller's sea cow, were named for Georg Steller. A scientist on Bering's 1741 expedition, he described all these animals in his writings.

## Europeans Come Ashore

For centuries the rest of the world knew little or nothing about the world of these Native peoples. That began to change after a Danish sea captain named Vitus Bering led a crew and two ships to the "land to the north" in

1741. Sailing under orders from the Russian government, Bering and his men reached the Aleutian Islands and sighted the coast of Alaska. On the trip back home, Bering and many of his crew died from scurvy, a disease caused by a lack of vitamin C. A few survivors returned to Russia, bringing sea otter pelts and news that the area was bursting with fur-bearing animals.

In 1741, Vitus Bering, sailing for Russia, became the first European to discover the coast of Alaska.

The Alaskan fur trade became very important to Russia's economy. A Russian fur trader could earn three times a typical yearly wage with a single Alaskan sea otter pelt. Russia, by the late 1700s, had become the greatest fur-trading empire in the world.

In the beginning, the Native peoples were eager to trade with the Russians for useful tools made of iron and for other goods. Many of the first Russian traders had Native wives and families. But the Russians carried diseases that killed many Native people. In addition, the Russian fur companies treated the Native peoples harshly and forced them to hunt sea otters as far from home as California. By the 1820s, nearly all the sea otters along the coast had been killed off, and the Native population was suffering.

Near the present-day town of Sitka, the Russians established their main colony. The powerful Russian-America Company was granted rights by the Russian ruler to "all industries connected with the capture of wild animals and all fishing industries on the shore of Northwestern America." The Russians tried to keep their activities in Alaska a secret from other nations.

Between 1774 and 1793, Spain sent thirteen ships to Alaska to study the Pacific coastline. The Spanish never set up a colony, but they mapped much of the area. They gave Spanish place names to Malaspina Glacier, the port of Valdez, and Madre de Dios Island. Explorers from Great Britain, France, and the United States also started to take notice of the region.

British explorer Captain James Cook sailed into Alaskan waters in May 1778, hoping to find a northern shipping route between the Pacific and Atlantic oceans. Cook mapped much of the Alaskan coastline. He and his crew also carried away sea otter pelts. The crew made a hefty profit selling them in Chinese ports.

As word about Alaska spread around the world, more ships arrived. In the early 1790s, the British explorer George Vancouver carefully mapped the Inside Passage and became the first European to spy "distant, stupendous mountains covered with snow." He was describing Mount McKinley and the Alaska Range.

## Seward's Folly

In the 1800s, American fur traders began competing with the Russians. The Americans traded sugar, guns, and alcohol to the Native peoples. Some of the Native groups used the guns to fight against Russians. The Russians proved unable to settle the region in large numbers or maintain friendly relations with the Native peoples. Tlingit Indians killed many Russian settlers.

By 1835, American whaling ships based in New England were hunting whales as far away as Alaska. While hunting in the Arctic, New England whalers met Eskimo whale hunters and learned about hunting the bowhead whale, an excellent source of oil. Before the discovery of petroleum, whale oil was an important fuel used in the United States. New England whalers were the major suppliers. In 1865, near the end of the Civil War, the Confederacy (the Southern states that had seceded from, or left, the United States) sent the warship *Shenandoah* into the Pacific Ocean to hunt down New England whalers. In the Bering Strait alone, twenty whaling ships were sunk.

It was clear by the 1860s that Russia was unable to protect Alaska. Russia also had growing money troubles. The nation had lost a costly war with Britain and

In 1867, Secretary of State William Seward arranged for the United States to buy Alaska from Russia.

the fur trade was in decline. By 1865, Russian rulers were interested in selling off Alaska and U.S. secretary of state William Seward was eager to buy it.

Most Americans knew little about Alaska and thought of it as a faraway frozen wasteland. They called it "Seward's Ice Box." They called the idea of buying it "Seward's Folly" (a folly is a foolish act). But in 1867, a deal was finally struck. The United States bought all of Alaska for $7.2 million, or about 2 cents per acre (0.4 ha). It turned out to be one of the biggest bargains in history.

Scrimshaw is an art form developed by Alaska's Native peoples. American whalers also widely practiced it. The Native scrimshaw artists scratched or etched fine designs onto walrus ivory, whales' teeth, or bones, and they colored the designs with dark ink. You can try your own version of scrimshaw art with materials from around the house or a store.

## WHAT YOU NEED

Piece of solid white plastic
  (try a yogurt or margarine lid)

Pen

Cutting board

Sharp nail or long wood screw

Black acrylic paint

Paint rag

Select a picture or design from a book or a magazine, or create your own design. Using the pen, draw your design onto the plastic.

Place the plastic piece on the cutting board and use the nail or screw to scratch the design into it. The tip of the nail or screw is very sharp, so you must be very careful. You should ask an adult to help you.

When you are ready to color your scrimshaw, place a drop of paint on the surface and rub it into the scratches. Clean the surface with the rag. When the surface is dry, you can add more details to your design and repeat the process.

## Quick Facts

### THE CALL OF ALASKA

Jack London (1876–1914) was an American writer popular especially for his stories of the outdoors. In 1897, he joined the rush for gold in Alaska and the Canadian northwest. He did not find any. But this rugged wilderness became the setting and inspiration for some of his best-known fiction, including *The Call of the Wild*, an exciting novel about a sled dog named Buck.

## Starting to Grow

Everyday life in Alaska did not change much in the first few decades after the U.S. purchase. Few people moved to Alaska from elsewhere in the United States. Congress made no effort to set up a workable government or regulate hunting and fishing.

William Seward, the secretary of state responsible for purchasing Alaska, was one of the first tourists to visit the region. He traveled there in 1869 and reported back on Alaska's natural wonders. The naturalist John Muir toured Alaska in 1879 and wrote about the beauty of the Inside Passage and Glacier Bay, calling it a "fairyland." In the 1880s, tourists began joining the small stream of fishers, miners, and other settlers who came to the area on steamships.

In the 1890 U.S. Census, Alaska's population was only 32,052. Of that total, 23,531 people, or 73 percent, were Native peoples. By 1900, however, the population had nearly doubled, to 63,592. The number of white settlers had jumped from around 8,500 to more than 36,500. The reason for the population increase was gold.

One of the biggest gold strikes in the region was made in 1896 along the Klondike River in Canada. By the following year, news of the strike had spread. To get to the site, herds of fortune hunters sailed the Inside Passage from Seattle, Washington, to Skagway, Alaska. Carrying a year's worth of food, clothing, and supplies, they then began a steep and dangerous trek over the St. Elias Mountains. The Skagway newspaper reported, "Miners in the Yukon require strong and rich food and they will drink bacon grease like so much water."

The search for gold also extended into Alaska, where some earlier strikes had also been made (for example, in Juneau in 1880). New strikes were made at

Some 60,000 fortune hunters were lured to Alaska in search of gold. One of the biggest gold strikes was in Canada's Klondike region. To reach it, people trekked through the Alaskan wilderness and over the treacherous Chilkoot Pass.

Nome in 1898 and Fairbanks in 1902. Once a discovery was announced, miners, homesteaders, merchants, and real estate dealers streamed in. More than 60,000 Americans traveled to or through Alaska during the gold rush. Many of them decided to stay.

## From Territory to State

In the early twentieth century, many of Alaska's mining and fishing camps grew into towns. Fur trading became less important, while gold and copper mining, logging, and fishing created many jobs. Roads, railroads, ships, riverboats, and telegraph lines were built to connect Alaska, in some degree, to the outside world.

But most settlements were still remote outposts, surrounded by vast wilderness. Roads were few, and mail and supplies had to be carried overland by dogsled. Margaret Murie, an Alaskan naturalist and author, described her childhood in Fairbanks: "We were all far away from the rest of the world; we had to depend on one another." On August 24, 1912, Alaska officially became a territory.

In 1917, the United States entered World War I, and many Alaskans joined the military. After the war, in 1922, Roy Jones, a former World War I pilot, flew a small floatplane from Seattle to Ketchikan. A floatplane is an aircraft designed to land in water and float. Soon, small airplanes, many of them floatplanes, were delivering mail and other goods over long distances throughout Alaska.

Quick Facts

## THE GREAT RACE OF MERCY

In the winter of 1925, the village of Nome was fighting an outbreak of diphtheria, a disease that caused many deaths, especially among children. Supplies of a vaccine to prevent an epidemic were low. No pilot was available to fly. A doctor in Anchorage arranged to have twenty mushers and their dogsled teams relay the vaccine to Nome, across 674 miles (1,085 km) of wilderness, with temperatures below −40 °F (−40 °C). The lead dog, Balto, became famous. Nome was spared. The rescue mission became known as the Great Race of Mercy. The dogsled race called the Iditarod is held every year in honor of the rescue.

Balto's fame spread far and wide. This well-known statue of the expedition's lead dog stands today in New York City's Central Park.

Alaska's population and economy grew during the 1930s, in part because of a jump in the price of one of the territory's two biggest products at the time—gold. The other major product was canned salmon.

World War II began in 1939. The United States entered the war in 1941, after Japan attacked the U.S. Navy base at Pearl Harbor, Hawaii. In 1942, Japanese planes bombed Dutch Harbor, on the Aleutian Islands. Japanese troops occupied two of the islands for a year, before being driven out.

During World War II (1939–1945), Alaska became important as a military site, known to many as the "Guardian of the North." President Franklin D. Roosevelt ordered fuel pipelines, airfields, military bases, and roads to be built. Among these projects, U.S. soldiers in 1942 built a highway running some 1,400 miles (2,300 km), from Dawson Creek, British Columbia, to Delta Junction, near Fairbanks, Alaska. Known as the Alaska-Canada, or Alcan, Highway, it was finished in just eight months.

Alaska continued to be important to the country's defense after the war, as tensions grew between the United States and the Soviet Union (a country that existed from 1922 to 1991 and that included Russia). Roads, pipelines, docks, railroads, and airports were built, and Alaska boomed. Families joined the workers, and soon there were many new houses, churches, and schools. The new Alaskans helped breathe life into a growing movement in favor of statehood. Despite some opposition in Congress, the necessary legislation was finally passed in 1958. On January 3, 1959, Alaska became the forty-ninth U.S. state.

## In Their Own Words

*We Alaskans believe— passionately—that American citizenship is the most precious possession in the world. Hence we want it in full measure. . . . We demand equality with all other Americans, and the liberties, long denied us, that go with it.*

—Territorial governor Ernest Gruening, calling in 1955 for Alaska to be made a state

# Energy and the Environment

Logging, fishing, mining, and tourism were the new state's major industries. Then, in 1968, huge deposits of oil and natural gas were discovered on Alaska's North Slope. The 800-mile (1,300-km) Trans-Alaska Pipeline, begun in 1975, was completed in 1977. It now carries oil across Alaska, from Prudhoe Bay in the north to the southern port of Valdez on Prince William Sound. There, oil tankers transport it to the lower forty-eight states.

Some 70,000 people worked on building the pipeline. The state has grown wealthy selling oil. Oil revenues pay for most of the state budget. In addition, each Alaska resident receives an annual cash dividend. In 2010, it amounted to about $1,300.

## Quick Facts

### THE GREAT ALASKAN EARTHQUAKE

On March 27, 1964, an earthquake struck in Prince William Sound, off the southern coast of Alaska. It caused a huge sea wave, or tsunami. The quake was the second strongest ever recorded at the time. Partly because the region was thinly populated, it caused less destruction and death than many smaller earthquakes. Still, there was heavy damage in Anchorage and over a wide area of Alaska and beyond. A total of 115 people were killed in Alaska alone. Nearly all of them died as a result of the tsunami.

The Trans-Alaska Pipeline, completed in 1977, carries oil from the North Slope down through 800 miles (1,300 km) of Alaskan wilderness to the port city of Valdez.

Opponents of the oil pipeline project were worried about its impact on the environment. Some of their fears were realized in 1989. That year, the supertanker *Exxon Valdez*, en route to California, ran aground and spilled nearly 11 million gallons (41 million liters) of its oily cargo into the clean, clear waters of Prince William Sound. Damage from the disaster continues to this day.

In 1980, the U.S. Congress passed a law that protected more than 100 million acres (40 million ha) of Alaskan land as national parks, wildlife refuges, and wilderness areas. Environmentalists hailed the action. Opponents argued that too much of Alaska's land was being closed to commercial development.

The 1980 law left open the question of whether to allow oil drilling in a certain area of the Arctic National Wildlife Refuge (ANWR). Those in favor of drilling argued that the oil would greatly benefit Alaska's and the country's economy and reduce the need for the United States to import oil from other countries. Many Alaskans also favored plans to build a gas pipeline from the North Slope, so that its natural gas deposits could be brought to market.

Opponents argued that the economic benefits in both cases were too limited and that the projects would seriously damage the environment. More than thirty years after the 1980 law was first passed, these proposals remained unimplemented and controversial.

Recovery efforts after the *Exxon Valdez* oil spill included using common dishwashing liquid to clean affected animals.

★ **c. 9000** BCE Traveling from Asia, the first Native peoples arrive in what is now Alaska.

★ **1741** Vitus Bering leads a Russian expedition exploring Alaska's coast.

★ **1778** British captain James Cook sails Alaskan waters, seeking a Northwest Passage between the Atlantic and Pacific oceans.

★ **1799** Russian fur merchant Alexander Baranov establishes the settlement of Old Sitka, in the Alexander Archipelago, and becomes manager of the Russian fur trade in the region.

★ **1867** The United States purchases Alaska from Russia.

★ **1896** Gold discoveries in the Klondike bring large numbers of people to Alaska.

★ **1912** Alaska becomes a territory.

★ **1942** During World War II, Japan bombs Dutch Harbor and occupies two of the Aleutian Islands.

★ **1959** Alaska becomes the forty-ninth state.

★ **1964** A powerful earthquake off the southern coast of Alaska causes a tsunami, killing 115 Alaskans.

★ **1968** Oil is pumped from a well at Prudhoe Bay, opening a new era in Alaska's economy.

★ **1971** The Alaska Native Claims Settlement Act is signed into law, granting the state's Native peoples rights to their ancestral lands.

★ **1977** The Trans-Alaska Pipeline, from Prudhoe Bay to the southern port of Valdez, is completed.

★ **1980** Congress passes a law protecting more than 100 million acres (40 million ha) of Alaskan wilderness.

★ **1989** The *Exxon Valdez* spills crude oil into Prince William Sound.

★ **2008** Alaska governor Sarah Palin becomes the vice presidential candidate of the Republican Party.

★ **2009** The 16-billionth barrel of oil reaches the port of Valdez.

★ **2010** Senator Lisa Murkowski narrowly wins reelection to the U.S. Senate as a write-in candidate.

# 3

# The People

Although Alaska is by far the biggest of the fifty states in area, it is the fourth-smallest in population. (Only Wyoming, Vermont, and North Dakota have fewer people.) Most of the population is centered in urban areas. More than 40 percent of Alaskans live in the city of Anchorage alone. Large areas of the "bush" have very few inhabitants.

Alaska has a large Native population, made up of Aleuts, Eskimos, and American Indians. About one out of every twenty Alaskans is Hispanic. Some African Americans who first came to the state as members of the military during World War II chose to live in Alaska after the war. Today, about 3 percent of the people are African Americans, and about 5 percent are Asian Americans. In all, about two-thirds of today's Alaskans are white.

Many Alaskans moved to the state in search of opportunity. Only about 40 percent of people living in the state today were born in Alaska. Those who have moved to Alaska in recent years have come mostly from other states. Only about 7 percent of today's Alaskans are foreign-born.

Whether they came to Alaska from somewhere else or were born in Alaska, people seem happy to be there. Many citizens never cross the state line. Those who do say that they are going "Outside." As one Anchorage woman notes, "We have a saying, 'Never come to Alaska while you are young, or you will forever spoil your eyes for the rest of the world!'"

Alaska offers plenty of recreational activities, including canoeing in Chugach National Forest.

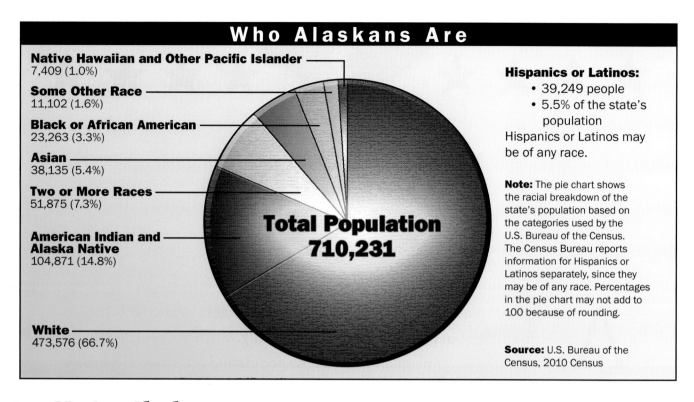

## Who Alaskans Are

**Native Hawaiian and Other Pacific Islander**
7,409 (1.0%)

**Some Other Race**
11,102 (1.6%)

**Black or African American**
23,263 (3.3%)

**Asian**
38,135 (5.4%)

**Two or More Races**
51,875 (7.3%)

**American Indian and Alaska Native**
104,871 (14.8%)

**White**
473,576 (66.7%)

**Total Population 710,231**

**Hispanics or Latinos:**
- 39,249 people
- 5.5% of the state's population

Hispanics or Latinos may be of any race.

**Note:** The pie chart shows the racial breakdown of the state's population based on the categories used by the U.S. Bureau of the Census. The Census Bureau reports information for Hispanics or Latinos separately, since they may be of any race. Percentages in the pie chart may not add to 100 because of rounding.

**Source:** U.S. Bureau of the Census, 2010 Census

## Native Alaskans

Before 1900, American Indians and Alaska Natives made up a majority of Alaska's population. Today almost 105,000 Native people reside in the state, making up a sizable minority. Some live and work in cities such as Anchorage and Fairbanks. There is also one American Indian reservation, for Tsimshian Indians, on an island in the Alexander Archipelago, off the coast of southeastern Alaska.

But many more Native people live in small rural villages. Often these can be reached only by boat or plane. Many village residents practice what is called a subsistence lifestyle. They hunt, fish, and gather or grow most of their own food. They often barter for goods and services, much as their ancestors did. They may trap furs to make clothing or other goods, and create art with materials they collect.

The traditional lifestyle has, however, seen changes. Hunters use guns rather than harpoons. Villagers travel by snowmobile instead of by dogsled. Fishers drive aluminum boats with outboard motors instead of paddling kayaks. Even remote villages have television service, telephone service, and Internet connections.

Alaskans of all ages and many different backgrounds gather to enjoy the annual Tlingit Indian Celebration in Juneau.

Village schools attempt to combine modern and traditional values. "Our kids participate in all the extracurricular activities," reports a Yup'ik village school principal. "They play basketball, race cross-country, and compete in the Native Youth Olympics. We even have a radio station!" At the same time, students learn the old traditions. "We teach subsistence classes in school," the principal explains. "The kids learn trap-building, net-making, boat building, all the traditional stuff you can think of!" There also are community programs

Tsimshian Indians raise a totem pole as part of a traditional American Indian festival known as a potlatch.

that coach children in traditional dance, song, and storytelling and teach Native crafts such as blanket-weaving, basket-making, kayak-building, wood and ivory carving, and beadwork.

## Northward Bound

Immigrants have always come to Alaska looking for better opportunities. The first Europeans in Alaska were Russians interested in trading furs. They built several outposts, and soon the Russian tsar (the ruler) sent missionaries to convert Natives to Christianity. The Russians built churches and set up schools for both Native and non-Native children. In Sitka and other parts of southeastern Alaska, you can still see Russian-style buildings and domed Russian Orthodox churches filled with gold artwork. Many town names in Alaska are Russian, and there are some Alaskans today who have Russian ancestry. But Russians never settled permanently in large numbers in Alaska. Most of the early Russian settlers left when Alaska became a U.S. possession.

The first large wave of arrivals to Alaska came in the late nineteenth century, after the Klondike gold rush. News of various gold finds had spread around the world. Fortune hunters poured in from faraway countries as well as from many parts of the United States and Canada. Each discovery of gold in Alaska brought an influx of people to remote and uncharted areas. When others followed to trade with the gold miners, the camps turned into boomtowns. The challenges that these newcomers faced were enormous. But their ability to survive

Russian-style churches, such as the Holy Resurrection Russian Orthodox Church in Kodiak, serve today as reminders of the area's first European settlers.

disappointment, sickness, hunger, bitter cold, storms, floods, and other hardships remains a source of pride to their descendants today.

Commercial fishing also attracted people to Alaska near the end of the nineteenth century. Fishers and cannery workers moved to the Kenai Peninsula and established the first factories in Alaska. As forts were established, American soldiers came and went. In the 1940s, the military set up permanent bases. The defense and transportation industries brought many jobs and new residents to Alaska. The population jumped from around 72,000 in 1940 to more than 225,000 by 1960.

The biggest spur to population growth was the discovery of oil, first on the Kenai Peninsula in 1957 and then in Prudhoe Bay on the North Slope in 1968. Oil field and construction jobs lured tens of thousands to the state. By 1990, Alaska's total population had reached more than 550,000. After 1990, population growth slowed, but most of the newcomers remained.

Alaskans, like all Americans, come from many different backgrounds and cultures. Many trace their ancestry back to northern Europe, including Germany, Great Britain, Ireland, and the Scandinavian countries. Other Alaskans have ancestors from Italy or Poland. In recent years, increasing numbers of immigrants have come from Asia and Latin America. Today, for example, Alaska is home to Hispanics from Mexico, Asians from the Philippines and South Korea, and Pacific Islanders from Samoa.

## Ernest Gruening: Politician

Born in New York City in 1887, Ernest Gruening became a doctor, worked as a newspaper journalist, and fought in World War I. But he is best known as the "father of Alaskan statehood." He worked hard for that goal, especially as governor of the Alaska Territory (1939–1953). Later, as a U.S. senator from the state of Alaska (1959–1969), he fought for equality for the state's Native population. He died in 1974.

## Carl Ben Eielson: Aviation Pioneer

Born in North Dakota in 1897, Carl Ben Eielson came to Fairbanks in 1922 to teach high school science. Soon after, he became a pilot, delivering mail and supplies to remote villages. In 1928, Eielson and a copilot were the first people ever to fly over the North Pole from North America to Europe. In 1929, he died in a plane crash while trying to reach passengers stranded on a ship along the Siberian coast. Eielson's heroism won him many awards, and an Alaskan air force base is named after him. He was inducted in 1985 into the Aviation Hall of Fame.

## Elizabeth Peratrovich: Activist

Elizabeth Peratrovich was born in Alaska in 1911, to Tlingit parents. After they both died, she was adopted by white Protestant missionaries. Moving to Juneau as an adult, she saw signs that said, "No Natives Allowed," and she began working to end discrimination against Native peoples. Her dramatic speech before the territorial senate in 1945 helped win passage of a measure granting Native peoples equal rights. February 16, the day the measure became law, is observed in Alaska as Elizabeth Peratrovich Day. She died in 1958.

## Susan Butcher: Dogsled Racing Champion

Born in 1954 in Boston, Massachusetts, Susan Butcher moved to Alaska at age twenty and began working with dogs. In the late 1980s, she became the first person to win the famous Iditarod dogsled race three years in a row. During her career, she was one of the race's top-five finishers twelve times. She died in 2006. In 2008, the legislature established Susan Butcher Day, celebrated on the first Saturday every March, as the Iditarod opens.

## Sarah Palin: Politician

Born in Idaho in 1964, Sarah Palin moved to Alaska as an infant. A high school basketball star, and later a mother of five, she served as mayor of Wasilla before winning election as governor in 2006. When Senator John McCain picked her as his running mate in the 2008 presidential campaign, she became a national figure. They lost the election, but Palin attracted many supporters, as well as many critics, and continued to be influential. She resigned as governor in 2009 but remained in the spotlight as a public speaker, author, and even reality-television star.

## Jewel: Singer and Songwriter

Born in Utah in 1974, Jewel Kilcher grew up in a remote area of Alaska. She says that the Alaskan wilderness became her greatest inspiration. Jewel sings and plays guitar. She also writes songs, yodels, and publishes poetry. She went through tough times to get her career started, but her talent and determination paid off. She has sold close to 30 million albums and performed all over the world.

## Cities and Villages

People living in Alaska's cities have a very different lifestyle from the way of life of people in villages or the remote bush. Yet all Alaskans live with the dramatic change of seasons and the incredible wilderness around them. For example, in Fairbanks, Alaska's second-largest city in population, drivers have an unusual problem in winter—ice fog. Ice fog is a thick, white, blinding fog made of ice crystals and automobile exhaust. But Alaskans are a hardy people. They know what to expect, and cope with these conditions as best they can.

Quick Facts

### ALASKA'S STATE UNIVERSITY

Most college and graduate students in the state attend the University of Alaska. Founded in Fairbanks in 1917, the University of Alaska enrolls about 33,000 students. The university is well-known for its Geophysical Institute, which does research in earth and space sciences and operates a rocket launch site near Fairbanks. Also well-known are its School of Fisheries and Ocean Sciences and its Supercomputing Center.

In some parts of Alaska, commuter planes fly to remote villages, carrying people and even delivering pizza.

The sprawling city of Anchorage includes Chugach State Park—a 500,000-acre (200,000-ha) wilderness area. That is not to say there are no busy city sidewalks and crowds. Anchorage is a beautiful modern city in the foothills of the Chugach Mountains, with museums, shops, restaurants, and theaters. It is a center for business and finance. Anchorage is also the location of the state university's largest campus. The University of Alaska has additional campuses in Fairbanks and Juneau.

Many Anchorage residents who prefer wide-open spaces have moved an hour or more drive from downtown. But rather than hop in their cars and head out on the highway, they often fly into work. "Almost as many people who have driver's licenses have a plane," says Wasilla resident Georgia Beaudoin. "People land their float planes on Lake Hood in downtown Anchorage; it's the busiest float plane terminal in the world!" More than half of Alaska's entire population lives in or near Anchorage, but the atmosphere still feels friendly and open.

Other Alaskans live in cabins in the wilderness and rely heavily on subsistence living. They may even lack sewers or running water. Many schools located in these isolated communities are outdated and cannot afford enough teachers or new textbooks. With few roads, people often travel by boat or snowmobile.

Young dancers celebrate their heritage at the Little Norwegian Festival Pageant, held each year in May, in the Alaskan city of Petersburg.

Goods must be flown in, which is expensive. Doctors and dentists are rare. People depend on health aides who can offer only basic care. Sick patients must often fly to a hospital some distance away. People living in villages count on one another to get by. "We look at family and community first," says a Yup'ik mother.

## Festivals and the Outdoors

Alaskans by nature have a great sense of adventure and fun, and their celebrations are full of lively variety. Many of them show off the heritage of a particular ethnic group. For example, every May, Americans of Norwegian descent hold a festival in Petersburg to mark the beginning of the fishing season. The Little Norway Festival offers boat tours, traditional Norwegian costumes and dances, and the array of Scandinavian foods known as smorgasbord.

Throughout southern Alaska, Native peoples host traditional celebrations called potlatches. Historically, potlatches were religious ceremonies that honored the dead. People sang, made speeches, prepared favorite foods of their ancestors, and gave away gifts. At potlatches today, people or events are honored with songs, dance, drumming, and sharing of foods such as fry bread and roasted pig. Participants also compete in fish-cleaning, net-mending, and tug-of-war contests.

Another popular event is the Native Youth Olympics, held each year in Anchorage. More than one hundred teams of Native youths compete in contests that reflect traditional fishing and hunting skills, such as the stick pull, knee jump, and seal hop.

About half of the world's 70,000 bald eagles live in Alaska. An annual festival in Haines celebrates their presence in the state.

One of the biggest festivals of the year is the state fair, held in Palmer. The Alaska State Fair is a ten-day event loaded with entertainment, contests, and exhibits. If you are hungry, you will find a variety of foods, from Mexican tacos to fresh Bristol Bay salmon. Another long-running celebration is the winter Fur Rendezvous in Anchorage, which honors the region's early fur trappers. During this winter festival, people enjoy ice sculpture displays and a variety of contests.

Nearly all of Alaska's festivals and events celebrate the outdoors. There are bird-watching events such as the Copper River Shorebird Festival, the Sandhill Crane Festival in Fairbanks, and the Alaska Bald Eagle Festival in Haines. At the Polar Bear Jump-off in Seward, contestants dress in silly costumes and leap into the freezing ocean. Other activities include a parade, ice bowling, and an ugly fish toss. In March, Nome holds the Bering Sea Ice Golf Tournament, during which golfers actually play a round of golf on the frozen sea.

Dog mushing is the official state sport, and throughout northern Alaska there are several major dogsled races. The most famous, of course, is the Iditarod. During the Iditarod, fans line the trail route from Anchorage to Nome and cheer on their favorite teams.

Though many Alaskans spend long, cold, dark winters playing indoor sports such as basketball, they would rather be outdoors. "You can't let the weather stop you," laughs a visitor to the Columbia glacier. Outdoor activities are boundless—Alaskans, and hardy visitors to the state, can ski, hike, cycle, drive snowmobiles, fish, hunt, kayak, sail, rock climb, camp, and more. And in the summer, when the days are long, people get outside as much as they can.

## ★ Iron Dog Race

Every year during February, participants compete in the world's longest snowmobile race. The course stretches more than 2,000 miles (3,200 km) from Big Lake to Nome to Fairbanks. For safety, riders travel in teams of two as they battle rugged terrain and harsh weather conditions.

## ★ Anchorage Fur Rendezvous

This event—often called the Fur Rondy—is held every year in February. It lasts into March, leading into the Iditarod. When it began in the early 1900s, it was aimed at giving trappers and traders a chance to show off and sell their wares. Today, the Fur Rondy includes about one hundred separate contests and other events, from a reindeer run and "frostbite foot race" to a "miners and trappers ball."

## ★ Iditarod Sled-Dog Race

On the first Saturday in March, mushers and their dogsled teams line up in Anchorage, in south-central Alaska, to start the race to Nome on the coast of the Bering Sea. They travel more than 1,150 miles (1,850 km), following a route used in the past to deliver mail and supplies by dogsled. Fans cheer along the way and at the finish line. Participants also enjoy arts and crafts exhibitions, music, dancing, and a reindeer potluck meal.

## ★ Mayor's Marathon

Racers flock to Anchorage every year on a day near the beginning of summer to run in the traditional 26.2-mile (42.2-km) "midnight sun" marathon. At this time of year, racers and fans alike are able to enjoy nearly twenty hours of consistent Alaskan sunlight.

### ★ World Eskimo-Indian Olympics

In mid-July, Native peoples from Alaska, the Pacific Northwest, and Canada come together in Fairbanks to compete in traditional athletic contests. Among the events are the high-kick, ear pull, blanket toss, and four-man carry. Other features include traditional dancing and a potluck supper.

### ★ Alaska State Fair

Every August, thousands travel by land, sea, and air to bring their vegetables, fruits, flowers, arts and crafts, and livestock to the fair in Palmer. There are delicious foods, games, fireworks, and concerts. Other typical attractions include a parent-child look-alike contest, a best scarecrow competition, a giant cabbage weigh-off, a pig-herding contest, and a joke and tall-tale festival.

### ★ Alaska Bald Eagle Festival

In November, birders and nature lovers from near and far flock to the Chilkat Bald Eagle Preserve in Haines to watch the world's biggest gathering of bald eagles feast on an end-of-season run of wild salmon. Other events include photo workshops, art displays, and the release of rehabilitated eagles back into the wild.

# How the Government Works

A laska became an official territory of the United States in 1912. However, as a territory, it was still ruled by the federal government in Washington, D.C. It did not have much control over its own affairs or any votes in Congress. The move for statehood gained momentum after World War II ended in 1945. A referendum in 1946 showed that most Alaskans supported statehood.

In late 1955 and early 1956, Alaskans held a constitutional congress and drafted a state constitution. The National Civic League called Alaska's constitution "one of the best, if not the best, state constitutions ever written." One admired feature of the constitution is that it does not attempt to achieve great detail. It leaves room for lawmakers to decide policies based on the current situation.

Alaska became a state in 1959. Like all the other states, big or small, Alaska has two U.S. senators. But, as one of the smallest states in population, Alaska elects only one member to the U.S. House of Representatives. These three lawmakers represent the interests of Alaska and its people in Washington.

Sitka was the first capital city of colonial Alaska, because it was where the Russian-America Company was based. But in 1880, shortly after the Americans took over, Juneau became the capital city. It has remained capital of the state of Alaska. Ringed by mountains and surrounded by the waters of the Inside Passage, Juneau is said to be one of the world's more beautiful capital cities.

Alaska's state capitol, in Juneau, was completed in 1931. It was used by the federal government before Alaska became a state.

# Alaskan Government

There are three levels of government in Alaska: city or town, borough, and state. Cities and towns are the smallest of these units. Alaska has about 150 cities and many more towns. Each is governed by a city council and by a city manager or elected mayor.

Alaskan boroughs, which are sometimes municipalities, are like most other states' counties. Each of the eighteen organized boroughs in Alaska is governed by an assembly and an elected mayor or a borough manager. These boroughs

Flanked by Mount Roberts, the modern-style Dimond State Courthouse, in downtown Juneau, was completed in 1974.

# Branches of Government

## EXECUTIVE ★ ★ ★ ★ ★ ★ ★ ★ ★

The state's chief executive officer, or governor, is elected to a four-year term. He or she may not serve more than two terms in a row. The governor oversees the various departments of state government, such as those responsible for education, natural resources, transportation, and public safety. He or she appoints the officials who run many government departments on a day-to-day basis. The governor can also approve or reject proposed laws.

## LEGISLATIVE ★ ★ ★ ★ ★ ★ ★ ★ ★

The legislative branch makes the state's laws, and it budgets the money needed to operate the government. There are two parts, or chambers, to the legislature: the house of representatives and the senate. The house has forty representatives, elected for two-year terms. The senate has twenty members, elected for four-year terms. There is no limit on the number of terms a legislator may serve.

## JUDICIAL ★ ★ ★ ★ ★ ★ ★ ★ ★

The judicial branch has four levels of courts. The superior and district courts hold trials in both civil and criminal cases. Their decisions may be appealed to the court of appeals and the supreme court. The five-member supreme court is the state's highest court. It supervises the other courts and can declare that a law violates the state constitution. Judges are appointed by the governor, from nominees selected by the Judicial Council. To stay in office after a certain period, judges must run for election. The Judicial Council monitors judges' performance and reports its findings to the public.

contain most of the state's population but take up only about 43 percent of the land area. The rest of Alaska is one huge, sparsely populated "unorganized borough," which is governed by the state.

In general, the state government is responsible for matters that affect Alaska as a whole. Transportation, the environment, business and economic growth, public health, and public safety are among the areas where the state has a major role to play. Like the federal government and other state governments, Alaska's government is made up of three branches: executive, legislative, and judicial. Each branch has its own responsibilities.

The governor's official residence is located in Juneau. It was first occupied in 1912 by the governor of the Alaska Territory.

## Native Claims and Corporations

During the days of European and American settlement in Alaska, no treaties were ever signed with the Native peoples. In 1924, Congress passed a law granting United States citizenship to American Indians and Alaska Natives, without taking away tribal rights and property. But the question of how much of the land the Native peoples had rights to was left unsettled.

In the late 1950s, the U.S. government began making use of what the Native population believed was its rightful land. The state's Native peoples formed a group to press for land rights. With the discovery of North Slope oil deposits in 1968, the issue became even more vital. In 1971, Congress passed the Alaska Native Claims Settlement Act, which gave the Native peoples ownership of a limited amount of land, 44 million acres (18 million ha), and a cash payment of close to $1 billion.

The act formed thirteen Native regional corporations and two hundred village corporations to manage the money and land. The corporations were made responsible for providing education and cultural services and for handling resources such as fishing, mining, logging, and oil drilling. Some of the corporations became very wealthy, especially those with oil on their land. All of them now play a key role in local government.

## How a Bill Becomes a Law

In Alaska, citizens can propose or change a state law without going through the state legislature. The process for citizens to make a new law by themselves is called initiative. The process for them to change a law by themselves is called referendum. In either case, they must collect signatures from other people in the state. If enough people sign, the initiative or referendum measure goes before voters in the next election. If a majority votes for the measure, it becomes law.

Most new laws or changes in Alaska's laws come about in a different way—through the state legislature. Each proposed law, or bill, must be sponsored by a member or a committee of the legislature. But sometimes lawmakers sponsor a bill at the suggestion of a citizen or group of citizens. For example, in 1997,

Sean Parnell, former lieutenant governor, became the tenth governor of Alaska when Sarah Palin resigned the office in 2009. He was elected to a full term in 2010.

first-grade students at Kalifornsky Beach Elementary, on the Kenai Peninsula, decided that Alaska should have a state land mammal. The students began by studying land mammals, and then they voted for their favorite, based on its importance to the history and culture of the state. The moose won the most votes. The students then asked their state senator to sponsor a bill declaring the moose the state land mammal. He oversaw the writing of the bill, which was given a number and introduced in the senate. It eventually became law. This is an excellent example of how Alaskan residents can become involved with their government.

In order to become law, a bill must go through various steps. Whether it starts out in the senate or in the house, it must first be considered by committees of lawmakers in that chamber. They may hold public hearings and make changes or additions to it. If and when the bill is approved by the needed committees, it is voted on by the full house or senate. The members may make more changes before voting. If a bill is approved by a majority of the members of one house, it moves on to the other chamber and must go through the same process.

Sometimes, the house and senate end up passing different versions of a bill. If neither chamber accepts the other chamber's version, a committee composed of members from both chambers tries to work out a compromise. The compromise bill must pass by a majority vote in both chambers before it can go to the governor.

Once a bill is passed by both houses in the same form, it goes to the governor. The governor can sign the bill, which makes it a law, or veto (reject) it. He or she may also do nothing, which means the bill may become law after a short waiting period.

A bill that the governor vetoes may still become law, but only if the two houses get together in a joint session and "override" the veto. A two-thirds, or in some cases a three-fourths, vote is needed to override a veto.

## Contacting Lawmakers

★ ★ ★ ★ ★ ★ ★ ★ ★ ★ ★ ★ ★

To find out which Alaska legislators represent your community, go to

**www.elections.alaska.gov/ vi_eo_state.php**

Click on "community name" under the heading Alaska State Legislature. When you find the name of your community, click on the letter or number link next to the name of the person you would like to contact.

## Quick Facts

### YOU NEVER KNOW

When Alaska voters go to the polls, the results can often be surprising. In a primary election in August 2010, Alaskans chose a little-known attorney named Joe Miller to be the Republican candidate for a U.S. Senate seat held by Lisa Murkowski. But then Murkowski decided to seek reelection as a write-in candidate. Although it was a long shot, she defeated both major-party candidates in November. She became the first senator elected by write-in votes in more than fifty years.

# Making a Living

With its farmlands, forests, inland and offshore waters, oil fields, and mines, Alaska has a wealth of natural resources to fuel its economy and provide jobs. Alaskans also work in factories, manufacturing goods that people buy. Many Alaskans make their living in the service sector of the economy. Some service workers are employed in schools, hospitals, stores, restaurants, or offices. Others are on the move driving trucks or tour buses or flying planes. Some work for the state or federal government, or for their own city or borough. In one way or another, they use their knowledge, skills, and energy to provide services that the public needs.

## Alaskan Farming

Farming seldom comes to mind when people think of Alaska, but there is close to 900,000 acres (360,000 ha) of farmland in the state. Most of it is in the Tanana Valley, around Fairbanks, and in the Matanuska Valley, northeast of Anchorage. Alaska's farmers grow hay, potatoes and other vegetables, barley, and oats, as well as greenhouse and nursery plants. Many farms keep dairy cattle, sheep, goats, or caribou. On the Seward Peninsula, Alaska Natives raise caribou for meat. Aleuts who live on the Aleutian Islands raise caribou and sheep.

There was some farming in Russian Alaska. After the United States purchased Alaska in 1867, American families could settle and acquire land for farming,

Passengers on a wildlife tour boat near
the Kenai Peninsula enjoy the view.

Farming is not Alaska's top industry. The long days of summer sun, however, help farmers grow vegetables, such as cabbages, to impressive sizes.

under the federal Homestead Act. But few farms succeeded because of the short growing season and high cost of transporting farm products to markets. When the Great Depression, a period of severe economic hardship, hit the United States in the 1930s, farmers in the Midwest and Great Plains suffered from drought, grasshoppers, and low crop prices. In a program set up under President Franklin D. Roosevelt, some two hundred farmers from Minnesota, Wisconsin, and Michigan settled in the Matanuska Valley. They got land and government aid to develop their farms and communities. Most did not remain. But the project helped bring in others who began to think of Alaska as a place to fulfill their dreams.

Although the growing season lasts only from June through September, summer days are long. With so much sun, Matanuska Valley farmers can grow truly giant vegetables. Alaskan farmers have shown off cabbages weighing more than 70 pounds (32 kg) and at least one stalk of Swiss chard that was more than 9 feet (2.7 m) tall.

# RECIPE FOR ALASKA WILD BLUEBERRY COBBLER

**Several different types of edible berries grow well in Alaska. In summer, Alaskans enjoy picking these wild fruits and use them to make jams, desserts, and other treats. Here is a recipe for a tasty berry cobbler.**

## WHAT YOU NEED

$^1/_2$ teaspoon (2.5 g) margarine

4 cups (600 grams) of fresh blueberries (or frozen unsweetened blueberries)

1 egg

1 cup (120 g) all-purpose flour

$^1/_2$ teaspoon (2.5 g) baking powder

1 cup (200 g) regular granulated sugar

$^1/_4$ cup (60 g) butter

Before preparing your cobbler, set the oven to 375 °F (190 °C). Be sure to have an adult help you.

Using a bit of paper towel, rub a 9-inch-square (23-centimeter-square) baking pan with margarine. Wash the berries and pick off any stems. Spread the berries over the bottom of the greased pan.

Crack open the egg and empty the contents into a small bowl. Beat the egg with a fork and set aside. In a medium-sized bowl, mix the flour, baking powder, and sugar. Add the beaten egg to this flour mixture and stir the ingredients until crumbly.

Spread the mixture over the berries. Dot the top with small pats of butter. Bake for 45 to 50 minutes. Ask an adult to help take the cobbler from the oven. Be sure to use oven mitts—the pan will be very hot. Cool the cobbler until it is warm but not hot.

Now your cobbler is ready to eat. If you like, try serving it with ice cream.

## Sea Harvest

Many Alaskans work in the fishing industry. Wild salmon are plentiful in Alaska. There are five types found in Alaskan waters. One is king, or chinook, salmon—which is the largest and most valuable variety. The others are sockeye, silver (coho), chum, and pink salmon. Crab are also caught in large numbers, along with shrimp, halibut, and bottom fish such as red snapper and ling cod.

Besides the fishers who go to sea, many other people work in fishing-related occupations. There are food processors who clean, ice, and prepare the fish for market. There are also jobs in shipbuilding and ship repair, gear and tackle manufacturing and sales, transportation of seafood, and sales of fish products. Some fishers sell their fish directly to customers on the Internet.

For several decades, the fishing industry has had ups and downs. And many jobs in the industry are only for a part of the year. Some fishers complain about competition from fish farms that raise salmon in pens. These farms can supply markets year round and are unaffected by weather conditions or breeding schedules of the fish. But many people who enjoy good fish say nothing tastes as great as wild Alaska seafood.

## Natural Riches

There are also plenty of natural resources to be found on land. Thick, green rain forests of cedar, hemlock, and spruce cover southeastern Alaska. Loggers have harvested timber in Alaska since it was a Russian colony. After railroads and shipping ports were built during World War II, logging companies were able to deliver lumber to markets around the world. Small coastal towns prospered from this increased business.

Only a small fraction of Alaska's forestland has been harvested for lumber. In recent years, many jobs in the logging industry have been lost. At the same time, environmentalists want to protect the state's unspoiled wilderness and the wildlife that live there. The federal government regulates logging on Alaska's public lands. It must try to balance the need for a healthy economy with the need for a healthy environment.

## A TOUGH JOB

Fishers have the most dangerous job in America, and Alaska's crab fishers are said to have the most dangerous job of all. They lower 700-pound (300-kg) steel crab traps, or "pots," into the rough frigid waters of the Bering Sea, and they spend long hours working on decks that are often wet or icy. Drowning, boat accidents, and overexposure to the cold are big risks. These workers' life at sea is the subject of a popular reality-TV series called *Deadliest Catch*.

Truckers brave the Alaskan cold to drive supplies long distances on remote highways.

Minerals provide Alaska with its most valuable industry. Important minerals include zinc, gold, lead, silver, and sand and gravel. Alaska also has large natural gas deposits.

Oil is by far the greatest moneymaker, however. The oil find that changed the face of modern Alaska came in 1968, when huge oil reserves were discovered on the North Slope near Prudhoe Bay. The oil field was twice the size of any other in North America. In 1977, Alaskans finished the 800-mile (1,300-km) Trans-Alaska Pipeline over the permafrost from the Arctic Sea oil fields to the port of Valdez. About 70,000 people in total worked on this construction project at some time, and they were well paid. Many decided to settle in the state. Today, the oil industry directly provides about 40,000 jobs in Alaska.

Once the oil began to flow, Alaska's treasury grew rich. Money from oil sales now supports about 90 percent of the state government's budget. Citizens voted to put some of the profits from oil sales into a special account called the Alaska Permanent Fund. Checks are given out each year to eligible Alaska residents for their share of earnings in the fund.

Alaska's oil production has declined by more than half since its peak in 1988. Many people want to boost production and create more jobs by drilling for oil in part of the Arctic National Wildlife Refuge on Alaska's North Slope. Others oppose drilling. They fear the impact of development on the unspoiled environment, especially on the life cycle of the caribou that migrate to the region each spring to bear their young. The federal government owns the ANWR, as it does most land in Alaska. The U.S. Congress will make the final decision on drilling in the area.

## Quick Facts

### THE LONG HAUL

Truckers bringing supplies to the Prudhoe Bay oil field drive along the Dalton Highway. It starts north of Fairbanks and stretches 414 miles (666 km) across the forests, mountains, and tundra of northern Alaska. The drivers brave frigid temperatures, high winds, and blinding storms. For most of the route, there are no gas stations, restaurants, or signs of human life. The story of these and other truckers is told in the popular reality-TV series *Ice Road Truckers.*

## Caribou (Reindeer)

Alaska's Native peoples have long relied on caribou as a source of food and fur. When the herds of wild caribou declined in the 1890s, missionaries imported them from Siberia to Alaska to help feed the Native population. Today, Alaska Natives still herd caribou on the Seward Peninsula and in other regions.

## Western Hemlock

The Western hemlock is the most common tree growing in the rain forests of southeastern Alaska. More than 200 feet (60 m) tall, this sturdy tree was once used to build mineshafts and railroad tracks. The Native population used it to make medicines. The hemlock is harvested for use in construction and for making high-quality paper.

## Oil

When people think of Alaska, oil is usually the first product that comes to mind. The discovery of huge oil reserves on the North Slope in 1968 was a bonanza for the state. Though oil output has fallen in recent years, oil still accounts, directly or indirectly, for one out of every three jobs in Alaska.

## Gold

Gold is the state mineral, and for good reason. Gold mining has a long history in Alaska. Alaska today is a major gold mining state, often ranking second to Nevada. During the gold rush days, miners rinsed out gold by sloshing ore and gravel around in goldpans. Some Alaskans still pan for gold along stream banks or the beaches near Nome.

## Alaska King Crab

There may be nothing to compare to the taste of salmon—Alaska's most important seafood product—but sweet-tasting, dark-red Alaska king crab comes close. Alaska crab fishers brave the rough waters of the chilly Bering Sea, often working twenty hours a day, to harvest their catch. Alaska king crab can weigh as much as 24 pounds (11 kg) and can measure 6 feet (1.8 m) from leg to leg.

## Mountains, Waters, Glaciers, and Woodland Trails

One of Alaska's greatest resources is the place itself. Close to 2 million tourists visit each year in the summer alone—to cruise, hike, fish, hunt, and enjoy the wildlife and scenery. They may arrive by ship or plane. They may drive the Alcan Highway, the only highway that connects Alaska to the lower forty-eight states.

## Alaska Works

Most Alaskans work in some kind of service job. They provide services to others by working as doctors, nurses, teachers, bankers, restaurant workers, truck drivers, firefighters, pilots, tour guides, and more.

Many Alaskans work in defense-related industries or are members of the military. More than 20,000 military personnel are stationed at early warning radar sites in the Arctic or on bases around the state. Alaska is home to two Army bases, Forts Wainwright and Greely, as well as Eielson Air Force Base near Fairbanks and the joint Elmendorf-Richardson base in Anchorage. These bases also employ many civilians.

Tourism is one of Alaska's growing service industries. From the Gates of the Arctic National Park in the north, to the Misty Fjords National Monument in the southeast, there is much to see and do. Tourists come to watch bears feed on salmon at Katmai Falls, ride the scenic railway at Skagway, hear glaciers break up in Glacier Bay, or see the Northern Lights in Barrow. They kayak, hunt, fish, bird-watch, whale-watch, hike, and more. More than a million tourists arrive each year by cruise ship alone, and more than a half million come by air.

Although the money from tourism is welcome, there are downsides to having so many visitors. The big cruise ships are like giant floating cities, and the crowds that pour forth can overwhelm some of the places they visit. Environmentalists are also concerned about the wastewater that ships dump overboard. To some Alaskans, tour buses and sightseeing helicopters take away from the peaceful

## Workers & Industries

| Industry | Number of People Working in That Industry | Percentage of All Workers Who Are Working in That Industry |
|---|---|---|
| Education and health care | 76,603 | 23.0% |
| Wholesale and retail businesses | 46,455 | 13.9% |
| Publishing, media, entertainment, hotels, and restaurants | 36,873 | 11.1% |
| Government | 32,540 | 9.8% |
| Professionals, scientists, and managers | 29,798 | 8.9% |
| Transportation and public utilities | 27,188 | 8.2% |
| Construction | 26,791 | 8.0% |
| Farming, fishing, forestry, and mining | 15,581 | 4.7% |
| Other services | 14,336 | 4.3% |
| Banking and finance, insurance, and real estate | 14,260 | 4.3% |
| Manufacturing | 13,039 | 3.9% |
| **Totals** | **333,464** | **100%** |

**Notes:** Figures above do not include people in the armed forces. "Professionals" includes people such as doctors and lawyers. Percentages may not add to 100 because of rounding.

**Source:** U.S. Bureau of the Census, 2009 estimates

The Alaska Railroad runs large domed passenger cars between Fairbanks and Anchorage.

beauty everyone came to enjoy. As visitors keep coming, communities, business leaders, and government officials are working to see that the Great Land can be enjoyed in all of its splendor.

Transportation workers are key to Alaska's survival. The state is huge and far away from the rest of the world's markets. Little food is grown locally, and few consumer goods are manufactured, so these items have to be brought in from outside. Truckers battle rough, lonely, frozen roads to deliver goods to remote towns. And many places where people live and work—including the capital city of Juneau and other southeast towns such as Ketchikan, Haines, and Skagway— have no roads from outside. Travelers get there by air or by sea, often on ferries operated by the Alaska Marine Highway System.

Railroads were first built to haul ore and timber and to serve the military. Now there is only one major railroad left in the state, the Alaska Railroad. It runs between Seward and Fairbanks. People wait alongside the tracks and flag the train to stop. This popular run is one of the world's last "flagstop" railroads.

Though costly, an airplane is often the best or only way for people to get supplies and services. Many Alaskans have pilot's licenses and own planes. A bush pilot said that in the early years of flight he flew "into areas that weren't even on the map. Every flight back then was a grand adventure." Alaskans, and visitors to Alaska, will likely agree that life in America's last frontier can still be a grand adventure.

An Aleut seventh grader named Benny Benson had the winning entry in a contest to design the Alaska flag. The Alaska Territory first adopted Benny's design in 1927. It has a blue background, the color of the Alaskan sky and the color of Alaska's official flower, the forget-me-not. Scattered against the blue are seven gold stars, representing the Big Dipper, the brightest stars in the constellation Ursa Major ("Great Bear"). The stars represent Alaska's strength. They lead to an eighth star, the North Star, representing the northernmost state.

The state seal was designed in 1910, when Alaska was still a territory. Inside a gold circle, it shows the Northern Lights glowing over tall mountains. The inside of the circle also has several images suggesting different sources of the state's great wealth, including a smelter to represent mining, a train and ships, timber, and a farmer with a horse and some wheat. The rim of the circle shows a seal and a fish, representing wealth from the sea.

# ALASKA

ARCTIC OCEAN •Barrow

RUSSIA

BEAUFORT SEA

Point Hope•
Prudhoe Bay•  •Kaktovik

Colville River

Alaska Maritime National Wildlife Refuge

BAIRD MOUNTAINS
BROOKS RANGE

Arctic National Wildlife Refuge

Cape Krusenstern National Monument
•Kotzebue

Kobuk Valley National Park

Gates of the Arctic National Park and Preserve

Yukon Flats National Wildlife Refuge

Porcupine River

Chandalar River
DALTON HIGHWAY

Koyukuk National Wildlife Refuge

ARCTIC CIRCLE

•Fort Yukon

Gambell•
Nome•

Koyukuk River

Yukon River

CANADA

BERING SEA

SAINT LAWRENCE ISLAND

Norton Sound

Yukon Delta National Wildlife Refuge

Yukon River

KUSKOKWIM RANGE

Denali National Park and Preserve

College•  •Fairbanks

Tanana River
6

Iditarod•

Mount McKinley Highest Point in North America

3

2

Bethel•

Kuskokwim River

ALASKA RANGE

Denali State Park

TAYLOR HIGHWAY

4

2

NUNIVAK ISLAND

Kvichak Bay

Wasilla•

WRANGELL MOUNTAINS

Wrangell-St. Elias National Park and Preserve

Lake Clark National Park and Preserve

Anchorage•
Kenai•

Chugach State Park

1

4

Valdez•

PRIBILOF ISLANDS

Wood-Tikchik State Park

Nushagak River

Iliamna Lake

Lake Clark

Seward•

9

1

Prince William Sound

Chugach National Forest

BERING GLACIER

SEWARD GLACIER

Chilkat State Park

Kachemak Bay

Homer•

Kenai Fjords National Park

Chugach National Forest

MALASPINA GLACIER

Yukutat•

Juneau

Bristol Bay

Becharof Lake

Katmai National Park and Preserve

Naknek Lake

•Kodiak

Glacier Bay National Park and Preserve

Tongass National Forest

GULF OF ALASKA

Sitka•  •Petersburg

Aniakchak National Monument and Preserve

Kodiak National Wildlife Refuge

KODIAK ISLANDS

Admiralty Island National Monument

ATTU ISLAND

ALEUTIAN ISLANDS

Dutch Harbor•

•Ketchikan

Alaska Maritime National Wildlife Refuge

Adak Station•

•Unalaska

ALEUTIAN RANGE

PACIFIC OCEAN

ANDREANOF ISLANDS

**Legend**

— State Highway
• City or Town
★ State Capital
▲ Highest Point in the State
▲ Mountains
🌲 National Park
🌲 National Forest
State Park
National Park and Preserve
National Monument
National Monument and Preserve
Maritime Wildlife Refuge
National Wildlife Refuge
Unpaved Road

miles
0        200

# Alaska's Flag

words by Marie Drake
music by Elinor Dusenbury

## BOOKS

Aretha, David. *Denali National Park and Preserve*. Berkeley Heights, NJ: MyReportLinks.com Books, 2009.

Benoit, Peter. *The Exxon Valdez Oil Spill*. Danbury, CT: Children's Press, 2011.

Doak, Robin S. *Subarctic Peoples (First Natives of North America)*. Chicago: Heinemann Library, 2011.

Locker, Thomas. *John Muir: America's Naturalist*. Golden, CO: Fulcrum Publishing, 2010.

Lourie, Peter. *Whaling Season: A Year in the Life of an Arctic Whale Scientist*. Boston: Houghton Mifflin Books for Children, 2009.

Petrillo, Lisa. *Sarah Palin*. Greensboro, NC: Morgan Reynolds Publishing, 2010.

Whitelaw, Ian. *Snow Dogs! Racers of the North*. New York: Dorling Kindersley, 2008.

## WEBSITES

**Alaska Native Heritage Center:**
http://alaskanative.net

**Official State of Alaska Government Website:**
http://www.alaska.gov

**Official State of Alaska Government Website for Kids:**
http://www.alaska.gov/kids

**Official State of Alaska Vacation and Travel Information:**
http://www.travelalaska.com

**U.S. National Parks and State Parks in Alaska:**
http://www.us-national-parks.net/state/ak.htm

*Ruth Bjorklund* lives on Bainbridge Island, a ferry ride away from Seattle, Washington, and two ferry rides away from Skagway, Alaska. She, her husband, and their two children plan to paddle their kayaks in Glacier Bay someday very soon.

*William McGeveran,* as editorial director at World Almanac Books, developed many editions of *The World Almanac and Book of Facts* and *The World Almanac for Kids*. Now a freelance editor and writer, he has four children who are grown up, and four grandchildren who will soon be old enough to read this book.

Page numbers in **boldface** are illustrations.